OCTOBER 50 COLORING PAGES FOR ADULTS RELAXATION

SHIH CHIEN HUA

PUBLISHED BY:
SHIH CHIEN HUA
Copyright © 2018

SEABIRD SHOP >50FOR

FB FAN PAGE

Disclaimer
The information contained in this book is for general information purposes only. The information is provided by the authors and while we endeavor to keep the information up to date and correct, we make no representations or warranties of any kind, express or implied, about the completeness, accuracy, reliability, suitability or availability with respect to the book or the information, products, services, or related graphics contained in the book for any purpose. Any reliance you place on such information is therefore strictly at your own risk.

OCTOBER 1ST

note:

_____

_____

_____

OCTOBER 2ND

note:

_____

_____

_____

OCTOBER 3RD

note:

_____

_____

_____

OCTOBER 4TH

note:

_____

_____

_____

OCTOBER 5TH

note:

_____

_____

_____

OCTOBER 6TH

note:

_____

_____

_____

OCTOBER 7TH

note:

_____

_____

_____

OCTOBER 8TH

note:

_____

_____

_____

OCTOBER 9TH

note:

_____

_____

_____

OCTOBER 10TH

note:

_____

_____

_____

OCTOBER 11TH

note:

_____

_____

_____

OCTOBER 12TH

note:

_____

_____

_____

OCTOBER 13TH

note:

_____

_____

_____

OCTOBER 14TH

note:

_____

_____

_____

OCTOBER 15TH

note:

_____

_____

_____

OCTOBER 16TH

note:

_____

_____

_____

OCTOBER 17TH

note:

_____

_____

_____

OCTOBER 18TH

note:

_____

_____

_____

OCTOBER 19TH

note:

_____

_____

_____

OCTOBER 20TH

note:

_____

_____

_____

OCTOBER 21TH

note:

_____

_____

_____

OCTOBER 22TH

note:

_____

_____

_____

OCTOBER 23TH

note:

_____

_____

_____

OCTOBER 24TH

note:

_____

_____

_____

OCTOBER 25TH

note:

_____

_____

_____

OCTOBER 26TH

note:

_____

_____

_____

OCTOBER 27TH

note:

_____

_____

_____

OCTOBER 28TH

note:

_____

_____

_____

OCTOBER 29TH

note:

_____

_____

_____

OCTOBER 30TH

note:

_____

_____

_____

OCTOBER 3ITH

note:

_____

_____

_____

OCTOBER 32TH

note:

_____

_____

_____

OCTOBER 33TH

note:

_____

_____

_____

OCTOBER 34TH

note:

_____

_____

_____

OCTOBER 35TH

note:

_____

_____

_____

OCTOBER 36TH

note:

_____

_____

_____

OCTOBER 37TH

note:

_____

_____

_____

OCTOBER 38TH

note:

_____

_____

_____

OCTOBER 39TH

note:

_____

_____

_____

OCTOBER 40TH

note:

_____

_____

_____

OCTOBER 41TH

note:

_____

_____

_____

OCTOBER 42TH

note:

_____

_____

_____

OCTOBER 43TH

note:

_____

_____

_____

OCTOBER 44TH

note:

_____

_____

_____

OCTOBER 45TH

note:

_____

_____

_____

OCTOBER 46TH

note:

_____

_____

_____

OCTOBER 47TH

note:

_____

_____

_____

OCTOBER 48TH

note:

_____

_____

_____

OCTOBER 49TH

note:

_____

_____

_____

OCTOBER 5OTH

note:

_____

_____

_____